AMERICAN HERITAGE

# BASEBALL
# GLORY

# BASEBALL
# DREAMS

WORKMAN 1993 PUBLISHING

Picture editor: Sabra Moore
Writer: Frederic D. Schwarz

Cover and title page: Baseball signed in 1950 by fourteen Hall of Famers, including Ty Cobb, Jimmie Foxx, Rogers Hornsby, Kid Nichols, Tris Speaker, and Cy Young.
Back matter: Box-office sign by Theo I. Josephs, ca. 1890

In the calendar grids are the names (and some portraits) of all the individuals who were inducted into the Baseball Hall of Fame through 1992.

*Calendars and diaries are available at special discounts when purchased in bulk for premiums and sales promotions as well as for fund-raising or educational use. Special editions can also be created to specification. For details, contact the Special Sales Director at the address below.*

Workman Publishing Company, Inc.
708 Broadway
New York, NY 10003

Printed in Japan
ISBN: 1-56305-163-X

# THE BALL

## BY ROGER ANGELL

It weighs just over five ounces and measures between 2.86 and 2.94 inches in diameter. It is made of a composition-cork nucleus encased in two thin layers of rubber, one black and one red, surrounded by 121 yards of tightly wrapped blue-gray wool yarn, 45 yards of white wool yarn, 53 more yards of blue-gray wool yarn, 150 yards of fine cotton yarn, a coat of rubber cement, and a cowhide (formerly horsehide) exterior, which is held together with 216 slightly raised red cotton stitches. Printed certifications, endorsements, and outdoor advertising spherically attest to its authenticity. Like most institutions, it is considered inferior in its present form to its ancient archetypes, and in this case the complaint is probably justified; on occasion in recent years it has actually been known to come apart under the demands of its brief but rigorous active career. Baseballs are assembled and handstitched in Costa Rica and Haiti (years ago the work was done in Chicopee, Massachusetts), and contemporary pitchers claim that there is a tangible variation in the size and feel of the balls that now come into play in a single game; a true peewee is treasured by hurlers, and its departure from the premises, by fair means or foul,

## THE BALL

is secretly mourned. But never mind: any baseball is beautiful. No other small package comes as close to the ideal in design and utility. It is a perfect object for a man's hand. Pick it up and it instantly suggests its purpose; it is meant to be thrown a considerable distance—thrown hard and with precision. Its feel and heft are the beginning of the sport's critical dimensions; if it were a fraction of an inch larger or smaller, a few centigrams heavier or lighter, the game of baseball would be utterly different. Hold a baseball in your hand. As it happens, this one is not brand new. Here, just to one side of the curved surgical welt of stitches, there is a pale-green grass smudge, darkening on one edge almost to black—the mark of an old infield play, a tough grounder now lost in memory. Feel the ball, turn it over in your hand; hold it across the seam or the other way, with the seam just to the side of your middle finger. Speculation stirs. You want to get outdoors and throw this spare and sensual object to somebody or, at the very least, watch somebody else throw it. The game has begun.

# 1 9 9 3 Y E A R A T A G L A N C E

## JANUARY
| S | M | T | W | T | F | S |
|---|---|---|---|---|---|---|
|   |   |   |   |   | 1 | 2 |
| 3 | 4 | 5 | 6 | 7 | 8 | 9 |
| 10 | 11 | 12 | 13 | 14 | 15 | 16 |
| 17 | 18 | 19 | 20 | 21 | 22 | 23 |
| 24 31 | 25 | 26 | 27 | 28 | 29 | 30 |

## FEBRUARY
| S | M | T | W | T | F | S |
|---|---|---|---|---|---|---|
|   | 1 | 2 | 3 | 4 | 5 | 6 |
| 7 | 8 | 9 | 10 | 11 | 12 | 13 |
| 14 | 15 | 16 | 17 | 18 | 19 | 20 |
| 21 | 22 | 23 | 24 | 25 | 26 | 27 |
| 28 |   |   |   |   |   |   |

## MARCH
| S | M | T | W | T | F | S |
|---|---|---|---|---|---|---|
|   | 1 | 2 | 3 | 4 | 5 | 6 |
| 7 | 8 | 9 | 10 | 11 | 12 | 13 |
| 14 | 15 | 16 | 17 | 18 | 19 | 20 |
| 21 | 22 | 23 | 24 | 25 | 26 | 27 |
| 28 | 29 | 30 | 31 |   |   |   |

## APRIL
| S | M | T | W | T | F | S |
|---|---|---|---|---|---|---|
|   |   |   |   | 1 | 2 | 3 |
| 4 | 5 | 6 | 7 | 8 | 9 | 10 |
| 11 | 12 | 13 | 14 | 15 | 16 | 17 |
| 18 | 19 | 20 | 21 | 22 | 23 | 24 |
| 25 | 26 | 27 | 28 | 29 | 30 |   |

## MAY
| S | M | T | W | T | F | S |
|---|---|---|---|---|---|---|
|   |   |   |   |   |   | 1 |
| 2 | 3 | 4 | 5 | 6 | 7 | 8 |
| 9 | 10 | 11 | 12 | 13 | 14 | 15 |
| 16 | 17 | 18 | 19 | 20 | 21 | 22 |
| 23 30 | 24 31 | 25 | 26 | 27 | 28 | 29 |

## JUNE
| S | M | T | W | T | F | S |
|---|---|---|---|---|---|---|
|   |   | 1 | 2 | 3 | 4 | 5 |
| 6 | 7 | 8 | 9 | 10 | 11 | 12 |
| 13 | 14 | 15 | 16 | 17 | 18 | 19 |
| 20 | 21 | 22 | 23 | 24 | 25 | 26 |
| 27 | 28 | 29 | 30 |   |   |   |

## JULY
| S | M | T | W | T | F | S |
|---|---|---|---|---|---|---|
|   |   |   |   | 1 | 2 | 3 |
| 4 | 5 | 6 | 7 | 8 | 9 | 10 |
| 11 | 12 | 13 | 14 | 15 | 16 | 17 |
| 18 | 19 | 20 | 21 | 22 | 23 | 24 |
| 25 | 26 | 27 | 28 | 29 | 30 | 31 |

## AUGUST
| S | M | T | W | T | F | S |
|---|---|---|---|---|---|---|
| 1 | 2 | 3 | 4 | 5 | 6 | 7 |
| 8 | 9 | 10 | 11 | 12 | 13 | 14 |
| 15 | 16 | 17 | 18 | 19 | 20 | 21 |
| 22 | 23 | 24 | 25 | 26 | 27 | 28 |
| 29 | 30 | 31 |   |   |   |   |

## SEPTEMBER
| S | M | T | W | T | F | S |
|---|---|---|---|---|---|---|
|   |   |   | 1 | 2 | 3 | 4 |
| 5 | 6 | 7 | 8 | 9 | 10 | 11 |
| 12 | 13 | 14 | 15 | 16 | 17 | 18 |
| 19 | 20 | 21 | 22 | 23 | 24 | 25 |
| 26 | 27 | 28 | 29 | 30 |   |   |

## OCTOBER
| S | M | T | W | T | F | S |
|---|---|---|---|---|---|---|
|   |   |   |   |   | 1 | 2 |
| 3 | 4 | 5 | 6 | 7 | 8 | 9 |
| 10 | 11 | 12 | 13 | 14 | 15 | 16 |
| 17 | 18 | 19 | 20 | 21 | 22 | 23 |
| 24 31 | 25 | 26 | 27 | 28 | 29 | 30 |

## NOVEMBER
| S | M | T | W | T | F | S |
|---|---|---|---|---|---|---|
|   | 1 | 2 | 3 | 4 | 5 | 6 |
| 7 | 8 | 9 | 10 | 11 | 12 | 13 |
| 14 | 15 | 16 | 17 | 18 | 19 | 20 |
| 21 | 22 | 23 | 24 | 25 | 26 | 27 |
| 28 | 29 | 30 |   |   |   |   |

## DECEMBER
| S | M | T | W | T | F | S |
|---|---|---|---|---|---|---|
|   |   |   | 1 | 2 | 3 | 4 |
| 5 | 6 | 7 | 8 | 9 | 10 | 11 |
| 12 | 13 | 14 | 15 | 16 | 17 | 18 |
| 19 | 20 | 21 | 22 | 23 | 24 | 25 |
| 26 | 27 | 28 | 29 | 30 | 31 |   |

# 1 9 9 4 Y E A R A T A G L A N C E

## JANUARY
| S | M | T | W | T | F | S |
|---|---|---|---|---|---|---|
|   |   |   |   |   |   | 1 |
| 2 | 3 | 4 | 5 | 6 | 7 | 8 |
| 9 | 10 | 11 | 12 | 13 | 14 | 15 |
| 16 | 17 | 18 | 19 | 20 | 21 | 22 |
| 23 30 | 24 31 | 25 | 26 | 27 | 28 | 29 |

## FEBRUARY
| S | M | T | W | T | F | S |
|---|---|---|---|---|---|---|
|   |   | 1 | 2 | 3 | 4 | 5 |
| 6 | 7 | 8 | 9 | 10 | 11 | 12 |
| 13 | 14 | 15 | 16 | 17 | 18 | 19 |
| 20 | 21 | 22 | 23 | 24 | 25 | 26 |
| 27 | 28 |   |   |   |   |   |

## MARCH
| S | M | T | W | T | F | S |
|---|---|---|---|---|---|---|
|   |   | 1 | 2 | 3 | 4 | 5 |
| 6 | 7 | 8 | 9 | 10 | 11 | 12 |
| 13 | 14 | 15 | 16 | 17 | 18 | 19 |
| 20 | 21 | 22 | 23 | 24 | 25 | 26 |
| 27 | 28 | 29 | 30 | 31 |   |   |

## APRIL
| S | M | T | W | T | F | S |
|---|---|---|---|---|---|---|
|   |   |   |   |   | 1 | 2 |
| 3 | 4 | 5 | 6 | 7 | 8 | 9 |
| 10 | 11 | 12 | 13 | 14 | 15 | 16 |
| 17 | 18 | 19 | 20 | 21 | 22 | 23 |
| 24 | 25 | 26 | 27 | 28 | 29 | 30 |

## MAY
| S | M | T | W | T | F | S |
|---|---|---|---|---|---|---|
| 1 | 2 | 3 | 4 | 5 | 6 | 7 |
| 8 | 9 | 10 | 11 | 12 | 13 | 14 |
| 15 | 16 | 17 | 18 | 19 | 20 | 21 |
| 22 | 23 | 24 | 25 | 26 | 27 | 28 |
| 29 | 30 | 31 |   |   |   |   |

## JUNE
| S | M | T | W | T | F | S |
|---|---|---|---|---|---|---|
|   |   |   | 1 | 2 | 3 | 4 |
| 5 | 6 | 7 | 8 | 9 | 10 | 11 |
| 12 | 13 | 14 | 15 | 16 | 17 | 18 |
| 19 | 20 | 21 | 22 | 23 | 24 | 25 |
| 26 | 27 | 28 | 29 | 30 |   |   |

## JULY
| S | M | T | W | T | F | S |
|---|---|---|---|---|---|---|
|   |   |   |   |   | 1 | 2 |
| 3 | 4 | 5 | 6 | 7 | 8 | 9 |
| 10 | 11 | 12 | 13 | 14 | 15 | 16 |
| 17 | 18 | 19 | 20 | 21 | 22 | 23 |
| 24 31 | 25 | 26 | 27 | 28 | 29 | 30 |

## AUGUST
| S | M | T | W | T | F | S |
|---|---|---|---|---|---|---|
|   | 1 | 2 | 3 | 4 | 5 | 6 |
| 7 | 8 | 9 | 10 | 11 | 12 | 13 |
| 14 | 15 | 16 | 17 | 18 | 19 | 20 |
| 21 | 22 | 23 | 24 | 25 | 26 | 27 |
| 28 | 29 | 30 | 31 |   |   |   |

## SEPTEMBER
| S | M | T | W | T | F | S |
|---|---|---|---|---|---|---|
|   |   |   |   | 1 | 2 | 3 |
| 4 | 5 | 6 | 7 | 8 | 9 | 10 |
| 11 | 12 | 13 | 14 | 15 | 16 | 17 |
| 18 | 19 | 20 | 21 | 22 | 23 | 24 |
| 25 | 26 | 27 | 28 | 29 | 30 |   |

## OCTOBER
| S | M | T | W | T | F | S |
|---|---|---|---|---|---|---|
|   |   |   |   |   |   | 1 |
| 2 | 3 | 4 | 5 | 6 | 7 | 8 |
| 9 | 10 | 11 | 12 | 13 | 14 | 15 |
| 16 | 17 | 18 | 19 | 20 | 21 | 22 |
| 23 30 | 24 31 | 25 | 26 | 27 | 28 | 29 |

## NOVEMBER
| S | M | T | W | T | F | S |
|---|---|---|---|---|---|---|
|   |   | 1 | 2 | 3 | 4 | 5 |
| 6 | 7 | 8 | 9 | 10 | 11 | 12 |
| 13 | 14 | 15 | 16 | 17 | 18 | 19 |
| 20 | 21 | 22 | 23 | 24 | 25 | 26 |
| 27 | 28 | 29 | 30 |   |   |   |

## DECEMBER
| S | M | T | W | T | F | S |
|---|---|---|---|---|---|---|
|   |   |   |   | 1 | 2 | 3 |
| 4 | 5 | 6 | 7 | 8 | 9 | 10 |
| 11 | 12 | 13 | 14 | 15 | 16 | 17 |
| 18 | 19 | 20 | 21 | 22 | 23 | 24 |
| 25 | 26 | 27 | 28 | 29 | 30 | 31 |

## JANUARY

| S | M | T | W | T | F | S |
|---|---|---|---|---|---|---|
| | | | | | 1 | 2 |
| 3 | 4 | 5 | 6 | 7 | 8 | 9 |
| 10 | 11 | 12 | 13 | 14 | 15 | 16 |
| 17 | 18 | 19 | 20 | 21 | 22 | 23 |
| 24/31 | 25 | 26 | 27 | 28 | 29 | 30 |

## 27
SUNDAY

## 28
MONDAY

## 29
TUESDAY

## 30
WEDNESDAY

## 31
THURSDAY

**MIKE KELLY
BORN 1857**

## 1
FRIDAY     **NEW YEAR'S DAY**

**TIM KEEFE
BORN 1857**

**HANK GREENBERG
BORN 1911**

## 2
SATURDAY

JOHN DOBBS (b. 1931) painted *Play at Third* in 1983 as part of a series depicting action at each base. He was a pitcher in high school and played on service teams while in the army during the Korean War. The players' and umpires' outfits in the painting are modern, but similar scenes have been generating excitement since baseball's earliest days.

# JANUARY 1993

## JANUARY

| S | M | T | W | T | F | S |
|---|---|---|---|---|---|---|
|   |   |   |   |   | 1 | 2 |
| 3 | 4 | 5 | 6 | 7 | 8 | 9 |
| 10 | 11 | 12 | 13 | 14 | 15 | 16 |
| 17 | 18 | 19 | 20 | 21 | 22 | 23 |
| 24/31 | 25 | 26 | 27 | 28 | 29 | 30 |

**3**
SUNDAY

**4**
MONDAY

**5**
TUESDAY

**6**
WEDNESDAY

BAN JOHNSON
BORN 1864

EARLY WYNN
BORN 1920

**7**
THURSDAY

JOHNNY MIZE
BORN 1913

**8**
FRIDAY

**9**
SATURDAY

**B**OB FELLER exhibits his form during the 1948 World Series. "Rapid Robert" did not have a good series, losing two games, but his Cleveland Indians nonetheless managed to defeat the Boston Braves 4 games to 2, to win their first World Championship since 1920. Loyal Tribe fans are still waiting for their team to do it again.

**JANUARY**

| S | M | T | W | T | F | S |
|---|---|---|---|---|---|---|
|   |   |   |   |   | 1 | 2 |
| 3 | 4 | 5 | 6 | 7 | 8 | 9 |
| 10 | 11 | 12 | 13 | 14 | 15 | 16 |
| 17 | 18 | 19 | 20 | 21 | 22 | 23 |
| 24/31 | 25 | 26 | 27 | 28 | 29 | 30 |

## 10
SUNDAY

HARRY WRIGHT
BORN 1835

WILLIE McCOVEY
BORN 1938

## 11
MONDAY

ELMER FLICK
BORN 1876

MAX CAREY
BORN 1890

## 12
TUESDAY

## 13
WEDNESDAY

## 14
THURSDAY

## 15
FRIDAY     MARTIN LUTHER KING JR.'S BIRTHDAY

JIMMY COLLINS
BORN 1870

## 16
SATURDAY

DIZZY DEAN
BORN 1911

**H**OWARD KOSLOW'S painting *Requiem—Polo Grounds* (24 by 37 inches) memorializes baseball's most idiosyncratic stadium. Below are seats salvaged from the polo grounds before its demolition in the mid-1960s.

# J A N U A R Y   1 9 9 3

**JANUARY**

| S | M | T | W | T | F | S |
|---|---|---|---|---|---|---|
|   |   |   |   |   | 1 | 2 |
| 3 | 4 | 5 | 6 | 7 | 8 | 9 |
| 10 | 11 | 12 | 13 | 14 | 15 | 16 |
| 17 | 18 | 19 | 20 | 21 | 22 | 23 |
| 24/31 | 25 | 26 | 27 | 28 | 29 | 30 |

## 17
S U N D A Y

## 18
M O N D A Y        MARTIN LUTHER KING JR. DAY        BILL McGOWAN BORN 1896

## 19
T U E S D A Y

## 20
WEDNESDAY

## 21
T H U R S D A Y

## 22
F R I D A Y

## 23
S A T U R D A Y

H ENRY CHADWICK was known as the Father of Baseball for his tireless efforts to promote and standardize the game in the 19th century. He invented the box score and the shorthand scoring system still in use; in addition, he wrote articles and issued pamphlets and guidebooks by the dozen. His 1888 *Base Ball Manual* shows the changes the game's equipment was undergoing at the time. Rudimentary gloves had been introduced but were not universally used; and while uniforms were getting to be less like dress clothes, the specialized athletic shoe was still years in the future.

# J A N U A R Y   1 9 9 3

## JANUARY

| S | M | T | W | T | F | S |
|---|---|---|---|---|---|---|
|   |   |   |   |   | 1 | 2 |
| 3 | 4 | 5 | 6 | 7 | 8 | 9 |
| 10 | 11 | 12 | 13 | 14 | 15 | 16 |
| 17 | 18 | 19 | 20 | 21 | 22 | 23 |
| 24/31 | 25 | 26 | 27 | 28 | 29 | 30 |

## 24
SUNDAY

## 25
MONDAY

## 26
TUESDAY

## 27
WEDNESDAY

## 28
THURSDAY

**GEORGE WRIGHT
BORN 1847**

## 29
FRIDAY

## 30
SATURDAY

THE NEW YORK YANKEES pull off baseball's most exciting play, the triple steal, as Billy Martin slides home ahead of the throw from Washington's Dick Brodowski in a 1957 game. Gil McDougald is the batter; the hapless Senators catcher is Ed Fitz Gerald. Martin would use the same sort of daring as a manager in the 1970s and 1980s with what became known as "Billy Ball."

# JAN / FEB 1993

**FEBRUARY**

| S | M | T | W | T | F | S |
|---|---|---|---|---|---|---|
|   | 1 | 2 | 3 | 4 | 5 | 6 |
| 7 | 8 | 9 | 10 | 11 | 12 | 13 |
| 14 | 15 | 16 | 17 | 18 | 19 | 20 |
| 21 | 22 | 23 | 24 | 25 | 26 | 27 |
| 28 |   |   |   |   |   |   |

## 31
SUNDAY

JACKIE ROBINSON
BORN 1919

ERNIE BANKS
BORN 1931

## 1
MONDAY

## 2
TUESDAY

RED SCHOENDIENST
BORN 1923

## 3
WEDNESDAY

## 4
THURSDAY

## 5
FRIDAY

HANK AARON
BORN 1934

## 6
SATURDAY

BABE RUTH
BORN 1895

**A** 19-year-old lefthanded pitcher with a live arm joined the Boston Red Sox in 1914. His tender age earned him the nickname "Babe." A couple of years later the official *Spalding Guide* noted, in something of an understatement, "Ruth is also an excellent hitter and can help the club with his bat." Those talents would not be fully displayed until he was traded to the New York Yankees in 1920, but in this 1985 lithograph Dick Perez commemorates Ruth's early days with the team that won the World Series in 1915, 1916, and 1918.

# FEBRUARY 1993

## FEBRUARY

| S | M | T | W | T | F | S |
|---|---|---|---|---|---|---|
|   |   | 1 | 2 | 3 | 4 | 5 | 6 |
| 7 | 8 | 9 | 10 | 11 | 12 | 13 |
| 14 | 15 | 16 | 17 | 18 | 19 | 20 |
| 21 | 22 | 23 | 24 | 25 | 26 | 27 |
| 28 |   |   |   |   |   |   |

**7**
S U N D A Y

**8**
M O N D A Y

**9**
T U E S D A Y

**BILL VEECK
BORN 1914**

**10**
W E D N E S D A Y

**BILLY EVANS
BORN 1884**

**11**
T H U R S D A Y

**12**
F R I D A Y      **LINCOLN'S BIRTHDAY**

**CHICK HAFEY
BORN 1903**

**13**
S A T U R D A Y

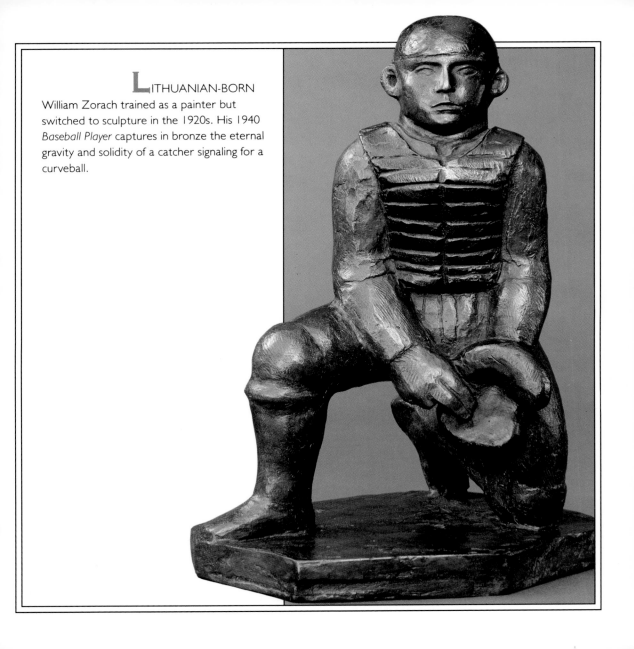

**L**ITHUANIAN-BORN
William Zorach trained as a painter but
switched to sculpture in the 1920s. His 1940
*Baseball Player* captures in bronze the eternal
gravity and solidity of a catcher signaling for a
curveball.

# FEBRUARY 1993

| FEBRUARY | | | | | | |
|---|---|---|---|---|---|---|
| S | M | T | W | T | F | S |
| | 1 | 2 | 3 | 4 | 5 | 6 |
| 7 | 8 | 9 | 10 | 11 | 12 | 13 |
| 14 | 15 | 16 | 17 | 18 | 19 | 20 |
| 21 | 22 | 23 | 24 | 25 | 26 | 27 |
| 28 | | | | | | |

## 14
SUNDAY          VALENTINE'S DAY

## 15
MONDAY          PRESIDENTS DAY

## 16
TUESDAY                                    BILLY HAMILTON
                                           BORN 1866

## 17
WEDNESDAY

## 18
THURSDAY

## 19
FRIDAY                          HERB PENNOCK
                                BORN 1894

## 20
SATURDAY                        SAM RICE
                                BORN 1890

Reach

BASEBALL GOODS

Get this one! "EASY TO BREAK-IN"

Get this too! "HARD TO WEAR OUT"

**A** 1910 store counter display advertises the snug-fitting gloves of the day, tiny by modern standards. The Reach company was founded by Alfred Reach, one of the game's earliest professionals, who (like his rival Albert Spalding) parlayed his diamond fame into a successful sporting-goods empire. Reach was also cofounder and president of the Philadelphia Phillies and part-owner of the Philadelphia Athletics.

# FEBRUARY 1993

## FEBRUARY

| S | M | T | W | T | F | S |
|---|---|---|---|---|---|---|
|   | 1 | 2 | 3 | 4 | 5 | 6 |
| 7 | 8 | 9 | 10 | 11 | 12 | 13 |
| 14 | 15 | 16 | 17 | 18 | 19 | 20 |
| 21 | 22 | 23 | 24 | 25 | 26 | 27 |
| 28 |   |   |   |   |   |   |

## 21
SUNDAY

**TOM YAWKEY
BORN 1903**

## 22
MONDAY

**WASHINGTON'S BIRTHDAY**

**BILL KLEM
BORN 1874**

## 23
TUESDAY

**HONUS WAGNER
BORN 1874**

## 24
WEDNESDAY

**ASH WEDNESDAY**

## 25
THURSDAY

**MONTE IRVIN
BORN 1919**

## 26
FRIDAY

**GROVER
CLEVELAND
ALEXANDER
BORN 1887**

## 27
SATURDAY

IN Marie Keegan's *Franklin Hardyston Miners Up at Bat* (1986), the outfield of a youth-league team plays shallow against a weak hitter. With proper equipment, umpires, and lights, the game played by youngsters has progressed considerably since sandlot days—but is the fence around the field meant to protect parents from stray foul balls or to keep them from meddling?

**MARCH**

| S | M | T | W | T | F | S |
|---|---|---|---|---|---|---|
| | | 1 | 2 | 3 | 4 | 5 | 6 |
| 7 | 8 | 9 | 10 | 11 | 12 | 13 |
| 14 | 15 | 16 | 17 | 18 | 19 | 20 |
| 21 | 22 | 23 | 24 | 25 | 26 | 27 |
| 28 | 29 | 30 | 31 | | | |

## 28
SUNDAY

## 1
MONDAY

## 2
TUESDAY

MEL OTT
BORN 1909

## 3
WEDNESDAY

JOHN MONTGOMERY WARD
BORN 1860

WILLIE KEELER
BORN 1872

## 4
THURSDAY

DAZZY VANCE
BORN 1891

## 5
FRIDAY

SAM THOMPSON
BORN 1860

## 6
SATURDAY

LEFTY GROVE
BORN 1900

WILLIE STARGELL
BORN 1940

COBB DETROIT

THE 1910 "Turkey Red" series of baseball cards, six-by-eight-inch whoppers that were obtained by redeeming cigarette coupons, are often said to be the most beautiful set ever produced. Ty Cobb was just 23 at the time, but he had already led the American League in both batting average and RBIs three straight seasons, making his card very desirable.

# M A R C H   1 9 9 3

## MARCH

| S | M | T | W | T | F | S |
|---|---|---|---|---|---|---|
|   | 1 | 2 | 3 | 4 | 5 | 6 |
| 7 | 8 | 9 | 10 | 11 | 12 | 13 |
| 14 | 15 | 16 | 17 | 18 | 19 | 20 |
| 21 | 22 | 23 | 24 | 25 | 26 | 27 |
| 28 | 29 | 30 | 31 |   |   |   |

**7**
SUNDAY

**8**
MONDAY

**9**
TUESDAY

ARKY VAUGHAN
BORN 1912

**10**
WEDNESDAY

**11**
THURSDAY

**12**
FRIDAY

**13**
SATURDAY

HOME RUN BAKER
BORN 1886

**S**CORECARD sketches portray handsome pitcher Tony Mullane (known as "The Apollo of the Box") and third baseman Warren "Hick" Carpenter of the American Association's Cincinnati Reds, and a trio of figures from Detroit's 1897 International League club.

| MARCH | | | | | | |
|---|---|---|---|---|---|---|
| S | M | T | W | T | F | S |
| | 1 | 2 | 3 | 4 | 5 | 6 |
| 7 | 8 | 9 | 10 | 11 | 12 | 13 |
| 14 | 15 | 16 | 17 | 18 | 19 | 20 |
| 21 | 22 | 23 | 24 | 25 | 26 | 27 |
| 28 | 29 | 30 | 31 | | | |

**14**
SUNDAY

**15**
MONDAY

**16**
TUESDAY

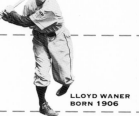

LLOYD WANER
BORN 1906

**17**
WEDNESDAY        ST. PATRICK'S DAY

**18**
THURSDAY

**19**
FRIDAY                                        JOE McGINNITY
                                             BORN 1871

**20**
SATURDAY

**N**ORMAN ROCKWELL'S *Game Called Because of Rain*, painted for a 1949 *Saturday Evening Post* cover, depicts a trio of grizzled arbiters (four-man crews didn't become standard until 1952) assessing the prospects for completion of a game at Ebbets Field.

# M A R C H   1 9 9 3

**MARCH**

| S | M | T | W | T | F | S |
|---|---|---|---|---|---|---|
|   | 1 | 2 | 3 | 4 | 5 | 6 |
| 7 | 8 | 9 | 10 | 11 | 12 | 13 |
| 14 | 15 | 16 | 17 | 18 | 19 | 20 |
| 21 | 22 | 23 | 24 | 25 | 26 | 27 |
| 28 | 29 | 30 | 31 |   |   |   |

## 21
### SUNDAY

## 22
### MONDAY

## 23
### TUESDAY

## 24
### WEDNESDAY

**GEORGE SISLER
BORN 1893**

## 25
### THURSDAY

## 26
### FRIDAY

## 27
### SATURDAY

**MILLER HUGGINS
BORN 1879**

The BALL that WON
THE WORLD'S SERIES

**A** 1920 advertisement rather implausibly attributes the National League's success in the previous year's World Series to its use of the Spalding No. 1 baseball. Subsequent developments revealed that gamblers had paid the Chicago "Black Sox" to throw the series, which may have had more to do with the outcome.

APRIL

| S | M | T | W | T | F | S |
|---|---|---|---|---|---|---|
|   |   |   |   | 1 | 2 | 3 |
| 4 | 5 | 6 | 7 | 8 | 9 | 10 |
| 11 | 12 | 13 | 14 | 15 | 16 | 17 |
| 18 | 19 | 20 | 21 | 22 | 23 | 24 |
| 25 | 26 | 27 | 28 | 29 | 30 | |

**28**
SUNDAY

**29**
MONDAY

CY YOUNG
BORN 1867

**30**
TUESDAY

**31**
WEDNESDAY

**1**
THURSDAY

HUGHEY JENNINGS
BORN 1869

**2**
FRIDAY

LUKE APPLING
BORN 1902

AL BARLICK
BORN 1915

**3**
SATURDAY

THERE must be a million people who swear that they were at Ebbets Field on October 3, 1951, when Bobby Thomson hit his "shot heard 'round the world." Memory can be deceptive, for the attendance was only 27,000—less than half capacity—and the game was played at the Polo Grounds. But no one who actually was there can forget Thomson's home run, which capped a four-run ninth-inning rally to win the playoff series for the New York Giants after they had trailed the Brooklyn Dodgers by 13 games in mid-August. And no one who listened on the radio can forget Russ Hodges' incredulous call of the blast and its aftermath: "The Giants win the pennant! The Giants win the pennant! The Giants win the pennant!..."

**APRIL**

| S | M | T | W | T | F | S |
|---|---|---|---|---|---|---|
|   |   |   |   | 1 | 2 | 3 |
| 4 | 5 | 6 | 7 | 8 | 9 | 10 |
| 11 | 12 | 13 | 14 | 15 | 16 | 17 |
| 18 | 19 | 20 | 21 | 22 | 23 | 24 |
| 25 | 26 | 27 | 28 | 29 | 30 |   |

## 4
S U N D A Y      PALM SUNDAY

TRIS SPEAKER
BORN 1888

## 5
M O N D A Y

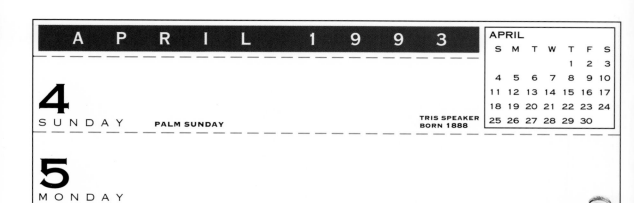

MICKEY COCHRANE
BORN 1903

## 6
T U E S D A Y      PASSOVER

ERNIE LOMBARDI
BORN 1908

## 7
WEDNESDAY

JOHN McGRAW
BORN 1873
BOBBY DOERR
BORN 1918

## 8
T H U R S D A Y

CATFISH HUNTER
BORN 1946

## 9
F R I D A Y      GOOD FRIDAY

## 10
S A T U R D A Y

ROSS YOUNGS
BORN 1897

New Haven
**Journal-Courier**
BEST FOR SPORTS

VS
AT
ON

THE symbiotic relationship between baseball and the press goes back a long way. Broadsides like this one, from around 1915, informed the public of the time and place of upcoming games between local teams—and, of course, promoted the sponsoring newspaper.

# A P R I L 1 9 9 3

**APRIL**

| S | M | T | W | T | F | S |
|---|---|---|---|---|---|---|
|   |   |   |   | 1 | 2 | 3 |
| 4 | 5 | 6 | 7 | 8 | 9 | 10 |
| 11 | 12 | 13 | 14 | 15 | 16 | 17 |
| 18 | 19 | 20 | 21 | 22 | 23 | 24 |
| 25 | 26 | 27 | 28 | 29 | 30 |   |

## 11
SUNDAY     **EASTER**

**CAP ANSON
BORN 1852**

## 12
MONDAY

**ADDIE JOSS
BORN 1880**

## 13
TUESDAY

## 14
WEDNESDAY

## 15
THURSDAY

## 16
FRIDAY

**PAUL WANER
BORN 1903**

## 17
SATURDAY

**ALEXANDER CARTWRIGHT
BORN 1820**

ONE CRITIC has written that John Marin's works "reveal influences of Whistler, impressionism, and cubism, as well as an intuitive sense of abstraction and expressionism." All these influences come through clearly in this crayon-and-pencil drawing entitled *Baseball,* completed in 1953, the year of Marin's death. It depicts a play at home and may be a reference to the blurry vision traditionally attributed to umpires.

APRIL

| S | M | T | W | T | F | S |
|---|---|---|---|---|---|---|
|   |   |   |   | 1 | 2 | 3 |
| 4 | 5 | 6 | 7 | 8 | 9 | 10 |
| 11 | 12 | 13 | 14 | 15 | 16 | 17 |
| 18 | 19 | 20 | 21 | 22 | 23 | 24 |
| 25 | 26 | 27 | 28 | 29 | 30 |   |

## 18
SUNDAY

SAM CRAWFORD
BORN 1880

## 19
MONDAY

DAVE BANCROFT
BORN 1891

## 20
TUESDAY

## 21
WEDNESDAY

JOE McCARTHY
BORN 1887

## 22
THURSDAY

## 23
FRIDAY

JIM BOTTOMLEY
BORN 1900

WARREN SPAHN
BORN 1921

## 24
SATURDAY

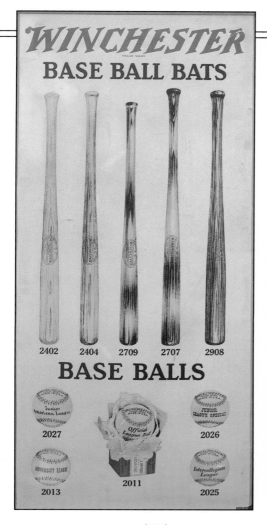

# WINCHESTER
### BASE BALL BATS

2402  2404  2709  2707  2908

## BASE BALLS

2027    2026

2011

2013    2025

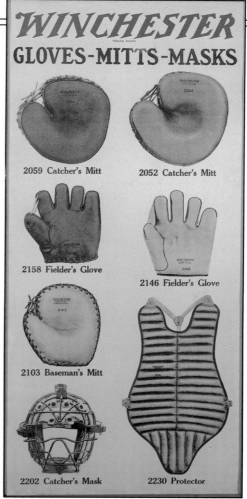

# WINCHESTER
## GLOVES-MITTS-MASKS

2059 Catcher's Mitt    2052 Catcher's Mitt

2158 Fielder's Glove

2146 Fielder's Glove

2103 Baseman's Mitt

2202 Catcher's Mask    2230 Protector

THE WINCHESTER company, best known for its rifles, manufactured other types of sporting goods as well. Two panels from a five-part 1930s advertising display, each 39 inches by 18 inches, show what the well-armed baseball team will have in its arsenal.

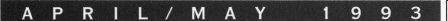
# APRIL / MAY 1993

**MAY**

| S | M | T | W | T | F | S |
|---|---|---|---|---|---|---|
|   |   |   |   |   |   | 1 |
| 2 | 3 | 4 | 5 | 6 | 7 | 8 |
| 9 | 10 | 11 | 12 | 13 | 14 | 15 |
| 16 | 17 | 18 | 19 | 20 | 21 | 22 |
| 23/30 | 24/31 | 25 | 26 | 27 | 28 | 29 |

**JOHN HENRY LLOYD**
**BORN 1884**

## 25
SUNDAY

## 26
MONDAY

**HACK WILSON**
**BORN 1900**

## 27
TUESDAY

**ROGERS HORNSBY**
**BORN 1896**

**ENOS SLAUGHTER**
**BORN 1916**

## 28
WEDNESDAY

## 29
THURSDAY

**LUIS APARICIO**
**BORN 1934**

## 30
FRIDAY

## 1
SATURDAY

THE young man in this turn-of-the-century portrait was clearly a baseball enthusiast, though it's unlikely that he actually swung the adult-sized bat he is posing with.

# MAY 1993

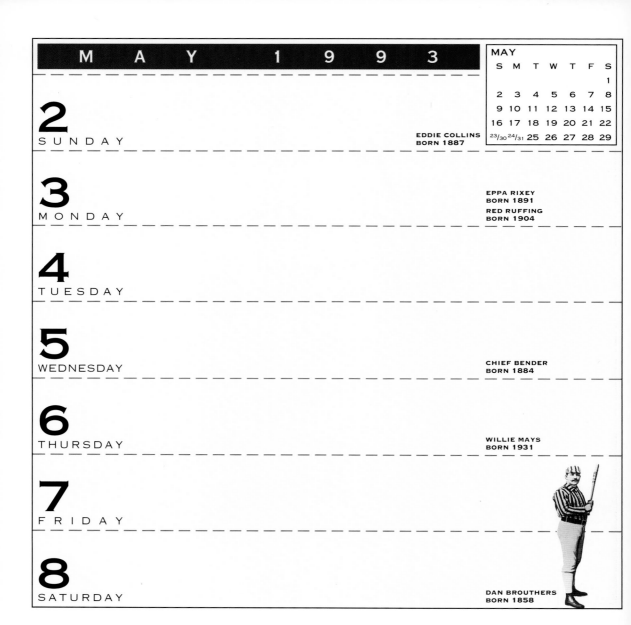

**MAY**

| S | M | T | W | T | F | S |
|---|---|---|---|---|---|---|
|   |   |   |   |   |   | 1 |
| 2 | 3 | 4 | 5 | 6 | 7 | 8 |
| 9 | 10 | 11 | 12 | 13 | 14 | 15 |
| 16 | 17 | 18 | 19 | 20 | 21 | 22 |
| 23/30 24/31 | 25 | 26 | 27 | 28 | 29 |

## 2
SUNDAY

EDDIE COLLINS
BORN 1887

## 3
MONDAY

EPPA RIXEY
BORN 1891
RED RUFFING
BORN 1904

## 4
TUESDAY

## 5
WEDNESDAY

CHIEF BENDER
BORN 1884

## 6
THURSDAY

WILLIE MAYS
BORN 1931

## 7
FRIDAY

## 8
SATURDAY

DAN BROUTHERS
BORN 1858

**B**ACK when World Series games were played in the afternoon, everybody in town, at work or on the street, found a way to keep up with the action. A painting from around 1950 shows fans following the series by newspaper, store window, radio, and the newfangled television.

# M A Y   1 9 9 3

| MAY | | | | | | |
|---|---|---|---|---|---|---|
| S | M | T | W | T | F | S |
| | | | | | | 1 |
| 2 | 3 | 4 | 5 | 6 | 7 | 8 |
| 9 | 10 | 11 | 12 | 13 | 14 | 15 |
| 16 | 17 | 18 | 19 | 20 | 21 | 22 |
| 23/30 | 24/31 | 25 | 26 | 27 | 28 | 29 |

## 9
S U N D A Y     **MOTHER'S DAY**

## 10
M O N D A Y

**ED BARROW
BORN 1868**

## 11
T U E S D A Y

**CHARLEY GEHRINGER
BORN 1903**

## 12
WEDNESDAY

**YOGI BERRA
BORN 1925**

## 13
T H U R S D A Y

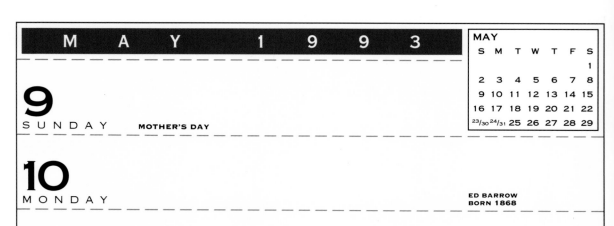

## 14
F R I D A Y

**ED WALSH
BORN 1881**

**EARLE COMBS
BORN 1899**

## 15
S A T U R D A Y

SEASON 1896

NEW YORK BASE BALL CLUB

THE JOURNAL

THE JOURNAL

HARRY M. STEVENS
PUBLISHER.

HOME PLATE.

Official Score Card

THE SCORECARD below shows the old (pre-1911) Polo Grounds in New York, with the Harlem River in the background; the fans' attire is not typical of the era.

K BASE BALL CLUB

FICIAL SCORE CARD

Publisher.

SEASON 1895

MEPHISTO AND ONDINA CIGARS ARE STRICTLY UP TO DATE.

Above is a less formalistic design from the following year. Both contain examples of an old baseball custom, corporate sponsorship.

# M A Y     1 9 9 3

**MAY**

| S | M | T | W | T | F | S |
|---|---|---|---|---|---|---|
| | | | | | | 1 |
| 2 | 3 | 4 | 5 | 6 | 7 | 8 |
| 9 | 10 | 11 | 12 | 13 | 14 | 15 |
| 16 | 17 | 18 | 19 | 20 | 21 | 22 |
| 23/30 24/31 | 25 | 26 | 27 | 28 | 29 | |

## 16
SUNDAY

## 17
MONDAY

COOL PAPA BELL
BORN 1903

EDD ROUSH
BORN 1893

## 18
TUESDAY

BROOKS ROBINSON
BORN 1937

## 19
WEDNESDAY

## 20
THURSDAY

HAROLD NEWHOUSER
BORN 1921

## 21
FRIDAY

EARL AVERILL
BORN 1902

## 22
SATURDAY

AL SIMMONS
BORN 1902

AN ebullient Lou Gehrig swings at a spring-training pitch in St. Petersburg, Florida, in 1932. He has reason to be happy, because he's coming off a season in which he collected 184 RBIs (an American League record that still stands) and tied Babe Ruth for the league lead in home runs with 46. Led again by Ruth and Gehrig, the 1932 Yankees would go on to win the pennant by 13 games and sweep the Chicago Cubs in the World Series.

# M A Y  1 9 9 3

**MAY**

| S | M | T | W | T | F | S |
|---|---|---|---|---|---|---|
|   |   |   |   |   |   | 1 |
| 2 | 3 | 4 | 5 | 6 | 7 | 8 |
| 9 | 10 | 11 | 12 | 13 | 14 | 15 |
| 16 | 17 | 18 | 19 | 20 | 21 | 22 |
| 23/30 24/31 | 25 | 26 | 27 | 28 | 29 |

## 23
S U N D A Y

ZACK WHEAT
BORN 1888

## 24
M O N D A Y

VICTORIA DAY (CANADA)

## 25
T U E S D A Y

MARTIN DIHIGO
BORN 1905

## 26
WEDNESDAY

## 27
T H U R S D A Y

## 28
F R I D A Y

WARREN GILES
BORN 1896

## 29
SATURDAY

GERALD GARSTON'S *Opening Day in the Minors* (1991) (54 inches by 48 inches) is a colorful tribute to the all-American game and its association with the flag. As the season begins, the idealized figures are seen before winning or losing, without wrinkles or grass-stained knees, and the air seems filled with optimism and hope.

# MAY / JUNE 1993

### JUNE
| S | M | T | W | T | F | S |
|---|---|---|---|---|---|---|
|   |   | 1 | 2 | 3 | 4 | 5 |
| 6 | 7 | 8 | 9 | 10 | 11 | 12 |
| 13 | 14 | 15 | 16 | 17 | 18 | 19 |
| 20 | 21 | 22 | 23 | 24 | 25 | 26 |
| 27 | 28 | 29 | 30 |   |   |   |

## 30
SUNDAY    **TRADITIONAL MEMORIAL DAY**    **AMOS RUSIE BORN 1871**

## 31
MONDAY    **MEMORIAL DAY OBSERVED**

## 1
TUESDAY

## 2
WEDNESDAY

## 3
THURSDAY

## 4
FRIDAY

**JACK CHESBRO BORN 1874**

## 5
SATURDAY

**A** 1910 FAN given out as a souvenir to ballpark patrons shows the captains of the 16 major-league clubs surrounding an excited distaff rooter.

# J U N E   1 9 9 3

JUNE

| S | M | T | W | T | F | S |
|---|---|---|---|---|---|---|
|   |   | 1 | 2 | 3 | 4 | 5 |
| 6 | 7 | 8 | 9 | 10 | 11 | 12 |
| 13 | 14 | 15 | 16 | 17 | 18 | 19 |
| 20 | 21 | 22 | 23 | 24 | 25 | 26 |
| 27 | 28 | 29 | 30 |   |   |   |

## 6
S U N D A Y

**BILL DICKEY
BORN 1907**

## 7
M O N D A Y

## 8
T U E S D A Y

## 9
W E D N E S D A Y

## 10
T H U R S D A Y

## 11
F R I D A Y

**ROGER BRESNAHAN
BORN 1879**

## 12
S A T U R D A Y

BUSINESSMEN have long understood the effectiveness of using baseball to sell their goods. Here a 1930s California firm pitches apples, and a citrus-flavored soft drink plays on the multiple meanings of its brand name. The boys in the illustration enjoy the baseball type of squeeze, but presumably they will soon become interested in the other variety, depicted on the bottle's label and at lower right.

SQUEEZE
— SCORES AGAIN —
*Flavors that please*

BEST STRIKE
BRAND
PAJARO VALLEY
APPLES
PACKED AND SHIPPED BY
MITCHELL MADESKO
WATSONVILLE, CAL.
PRODUCT OF U.S.A.
CONTENTS
ONE
BUSHEL

JUNE

| S | M | T | W | T | F | S |
|---|---|---|---|---|---|---|
|   |   | 1 | 2 | 3 | 4 | 5 |
| 6 | 7 | 8 | 9 | 10 | 11 | 12 |
| 13 | 14 | 15 | 16 | 17 | 18 | 19 |
| 20 | 21 | 22 | 23 | 24 | 25 | 26 |
| 27 | 28 | 29 | 30 |   |   |   |

**13**
SUNDAY

**14**
MONDAY

**15**
TUESDAY

BILLY WILLIAMS
BORN 1938

**16**
WEDNESDAY

**17**
THURSDAY

**18**
FRIDAY

LOU BROCK
BORN 1939

**19**
SATURDAY

LOU GEHRIG
BORN 1903

**A** patch from an 1870s quilt depicts two fierce-looking ballplayers. The mustaches they sport would briefly come back in fashion a century later, led by the ever-zany Oakland Athletics.

# JUNE 1993

| JUNE | | | | | | |
|---|---|---|---|---|---|---|
| S | M | T | W | T | F | S |
| | | 1 | 2 | 3 | 4 | 5 |
| 6 | 7 | 8 | 9 | 10 | 11 | 12 |
| 13 | 14 | 15 | 16 | 17 | 18 | 19 |
| 20 | 21 | 22 | 23 | 24 | 25 | 26 |
| 27 | 28 | 29 | 30 | | | |

## 20
SUNDAY    FATHER'S DAY

## 21
MONDAY

## 22
TUESDAY

CARL HUBBELL
BORN 1903

## 23
WEDNESDAY

GEORGE WEISS
BORN 1895

## 24
THURSDAY

## 25
FRIDAY

## 26
SATURDAY

BABE HERMAN
BORN 1903

**T**AGGED is the title of Oscar de Mejo's 1980 acrylic painting, but the tag must have come after the runner crossed the plate, because the umpire is calling him safe. He seems to have scored on a wild pitch or passed ball, because the man guarding the plate is not wearing catcher's gear. The runner's headfirst slide in such a situation is unorthodox but apparently effective.

# J U N E / J U L Y  1 9 9 3

**JULY**

| S | M | T | W | T | F | S |
|---|---|---|---|---|---|---|
|   |   |   |   | 1 | 2 | 3 |
| 4 | 5 | 6 | 7 | 8 | 9 | 10 |
| 11 | 12 | 13 | 14 | 15 | 16 | 17 |
| 18 | 19 | 20 | 21 | 22 | 23 | 24 |
| 25 | 26 | 27 | 28 | 29 | 30 | 31 |

## 27
SUNDAY

## 28
MONDAY

## 29
TUESDAY

**WILBERT ROBINSON**
**BORN 1863**

**HARMON KILLEBREW**
**BORN 1936**

## 30
WEDNESDAY

## 1
THURSDAY          **CANADA DAY (CANADA)**

**ROGER CONNOR**
**BORN 1857**
**JOHN CLARKSON**
**BORN 1861**

## 2
FRIDAY

## 3
SATURDAY

HIS NAME was Johannes Peter Wagner, but "Honus" was how everyone rendered it. "The Flying Dutchman" was not particularly fast, but by studying a pitcher's every movement, he was able to steal 522 bases over his 21-year career. During the 1909 World Series against the Detroit Tigers he stole six bases, including home, as seen above, leading the Pittsburgh Pirates to a seven-game victory.

# J U L Y  1 9 9 3

JULY
S M T W T F S
1 2 3
4 5 6 7 8 9 10
11 12 13 14 15 16 17
18 19 20 21 22 23 24
25 26 27 28 29 30 31

## 4
SUNDAY      **INDEPENDENCE DAY**                    **MICKEY WELCH
BORN 1859**

## 5
MONDAY

## 6
TUESDAY

## 7
WEDNESDAY                                  **SATCHEL PAIGE
BORN 1906**

## 8
THURSDAY

## 9
FRIDAY

## 10
SATURDAY

FROM the earliest days of commercial broadcasting, baseball and radio have helped each other prosper. Some clubs let stations air games for free just to get the publicity; others did not allow broadcasts for fear of losing customers. Nowadays radio and television rights can be the biggest part of a club's income.

# SCIENTIFIC AMERICAN
## The Monthly Journal of Practical Information

35¢ a Copy     MAY 1924     $4.00 a Year

BROADCASTING THE BASEBALL GAME. THE RADIO REPORTER AND THE RADIO ENGINEER IN ACTION

Scientific American Publishing Co., Munn & Co., New York

**JULY**

| S | M | T | W | T | F | S |
|---|---|---|---|---|---|---|
|   |   |   |   | 1 | 2 | 3 |
| 4 | 5 | 6 | 7 | 8 | 9 | 10 |
| 11 | 12 | 13 | 14 | 15 | 16 | 17 |
| 18 | 19 | 20 | 21 | 22 | 23 | 24 |
| 25 | 26 | 27 | 28 | 29 | 30 | 31 |

## 11
S U N D A Y

## 12
M O N D A Y

## 13
T U E S D A Y

**STAN COVELESKI**
**BORN 1889**

## 14
W E D N E S D A Y

## 15
T H U R S D A Y

## 16
F R I D A Y

## 17
S A T U R D A Y

**LOU BOUDREAU**
**BORN 1917**

**B**ORN in 1940 in Puerto Rico, the artist Dick Perez moved to New York City at age six. His love of baseball started with playing stickball in the city's streets. He is now the official artist for the Philadelphia Phillies and the National Baseball Hall of Fame. This uncut sheet is the first series of cards he produced for the Hall of Fame and includes portraits of inductees from 1936 through 1945.

# J U L Y   1 9 9 3

JULY

| S | M | T | W | T | F | S |
|---|---|---|---|---|---|---|
|   |   |   |   | 1 | 2 | 3 |
| 4 | 5 | 6 | 7 | 8 | 9 | 10 |
| 11 | 12 | 13 | 14 | 15 | 16 | 17 |
| 18 | 19 | 20 | 21 | 22 | 23 | 24 |
| 25 | 26 | 27 | 28 | 29 | 30 | 31 |

## 18
SUNDAY

## 19
MONDAY

## 20
TUESDAY

**HEINIE MANUSH**
**BORN 1901**

## 21
WEDNESDAY

## 22
THURSDAY

**JOHNNY EVERS**
**BORN 1883**

**JESSE HAINES**
**BORN 1893**

## 23
FRIDAY

**PEE WEE REESE**
**BORN 1918**

**DON DRYSDALE**
**BORN 1936**

## 24
SATURDAY

**TOMMY McCARTHY**
**BORN 1863**

THE BALLPARK was called Navin Field when William Harold Stockburger painted *Baseball in Detroit,* around 1930. It was renamed Briggs Stadium in 1938 and Tiger Stadium in 1961. Whatever the name, it has long been beloved by fans and is one of a dwindling number of classic ballparks. Unfortunately, it may be condemned to demolition by the time the last page of this calendar is reached.

# J U L Y   1 9 9 3

## JULY

| S | M | T | W | T | F | S |
|---|---|---|---|---|---|---|
|   |   |   |   | 1 | 2 | 3 |
| 4 | 5 | 6 | 7 | 8 | 9 | 10 |
| 11 | 12 | 13 | 14 | 15 | 16 | 17 |
| 18 | 19 | 20 | 21 | 22 | 23 | 24 |
| 25 | 26 | 27 | 28 | 29 | 30 | 31 |

## 25
SUNDAY

## 26
MONDAY

**HOYT WILHELM
BORN 1923**

## 27
TUESDAY

**JOE TINKER
BORN 1880**

## 28
WEDNESDAY

## 29
THURSDAY

## 30
FRIDAY

**CASEY STENGEL
BORN 1889**

## 31
SATURDAY

**S**PORTS AND SEX—an unbeatable combination—are used to sell a somewhat less exciting product, paint, in an advertisement from around 1920.

# A U G U S T   1 9 9 3

**AUGUST**

| S | M | T | W | T | F | S |
|---|---|---|---|---|---|---|
|   | 1 | 2 | 3 | 4 | 5 | 6 | 7 |
| 8 | 9 | 10 | 11 | 12 | 13 | 14 |
| 15 | 16 | 17 | 18 | 19 | 20 | 21 |
| 22 | 23 | 24 | 25 | 26 | 27 | 28 |
| 29 | 30 | 31 |   |   |   |   |

## 1
S U N D A Y

## 2
M O N D A Y

## 3
T U E S D A Y

HARRY HEILMANN
BORN 1894

## 4
W E D N E S D A Y

JAKE BECKLEY
BORN 1867

## 5
T H U R S D A Y

## 6
F R I D A Y

## 7
S A T U R D A Y

BILL McKECHNIE
BORN 1866

**G**IL HODGES makes a running one-handed catch of a foul pop-up off the bat of Wes Westrum in a 1954 game between the Brooklyn Dodgers and the New York Giants at Ebbets Field. Hodges had the best year of his career in 1954, with a .304 average, 42 home runs, and 130 RBIs. Despite his heroics, the Giants won the pennant that year and went on to sweep the Cleveland Indians in the World Series. Both Westrum and Hodges would later manage the New York Mets, Hodges guiding the formerly pathetic club to a World Championship.

# A U G U S T  1 9 9 3

| AUGUST | | | | | | |
|---|---|---|---|---|---|---|
| S | M | T | W | T | F | S |
| 1 | 2 | 3 | 4 | 5 | 6 | 7 |
| 8 | 9 | 10 | 11 | 12 | 13 | 14 |
| 15 | 16 | 17 | 18 | 19 | 20 | 21 |
| 22 | 23 | 24 | 25 | 26 | 27 | 28 |
| 29 | 30 | 31 | | | | |

## 8
SUNDAY

## 9
MONDAY

**BURLEIGH GRIMES
BORN 1893**

## 10
TUESDAY

## 11
WEDNESDAY

## 12
THURSDAY

**CHRISTY MATHEWSON
BORN 1880**

**RAY SCHALK
BORN 1892**

## 13
FRIDAY

## 14
SATURDAY

**T**HE ambience of baseball can be as fascinating as the action itself. In *Baseball Game* (1974) Ralph Fasanella depicts the preliminary rituals before a night game: players warming up, fans streaming through the turnstiles, umpires making small talk. One can almost smell the beer and hot dogs, and hear the expectant buzz of the crowd.

# A U G U S T   1 9 9 3

**AUGUST**

| S | M | T | W | T | F | S |
|---|---|---|---|---|---|---|
|   | 1 | 2 | 3 | 4 | 5 | 6 | 7 |
| 8 | 9 | 10 | 11 | 12 | 13 | 14 |
| 15 | 16 | 17 | 18 | 19 | 20 | 21 |
| 22 | 23 | 24 | 25 | 26 | 27 | 28 |
| 29 | 30 | 31 |   |   |   |   |

## 15
SUNDAY

**CHARLES COMISKEY
BORN 1859**

## 16
MONDAY

## 17
TUESDAY

## 18
WEDNESDAY

**ROBERTO CLEMENTE
BORN 1934**

## 19
THURSDAY

## 20
FRIDAY

**AL LOPEZ
BORN 1908**

## 21
SATURDAY

ALBERT
DORNE

**E**VER since its publication in 1888, Ernest Lawrence Thayer's *Casey at the Bat* has served as a paradigm for the inevitable disappointment that is every baseball fan's lot. Albert Dorne's painting *The Mighty Casey Strikes Out* portrays the denouement of the poem, as Casey generates a mighty gust of wind but fails to connect, stranding Flynn and Blake in scoring position to end the game.

# A U G U S T  1 9 9 3

**AUGUST**

| S | M | T | W | T | F | S |
|---|---|---|---|---|---|---|
| 1 | 2 | 3 | 4 | 5 | 6 | 7 |
| 8 | 9 | 10 | 11 | 12 | 13 | 14 |
| 15 | 16 | 17 | 18 | 19 | 20 | 21 |
| 22 | 23 | 24 | 25 | 26 | 27 | 28 |
| 29 | 30 | 31 | | | | |

## 22
SUNDAY

CARL YASTRZEMSKI
BORN 1939

## 23
MONDAY

GEORGE KELL
BORN 1922

## 24
TUESDAY

JIM O'ROURKE
BORN 1852

HARRY HOOPER
BORN 1887

## 25
WEDNESDAY

ROLAND GLEN FINGERS
BORN 1946

## 26
THURSDAY

## 27
FRIDAY

## 28
SATURDAY

**A**N 1844 painting by an unknown English artist shows a young boy holding a primitive bat and ball. The lad was no doubt fond of rounders, an early version of baseball.

# AUG / SEPT 1993

| S | M | T | W | T | F | S |
|---|---|---|---|---|---|---|
| | | | | 1 | 2 | 3 | 4 |
| 5 | 6 | 7 | 8 | 9 | 10 | 11 |
| 12 | 13 | 14 | 15 | 16 | 17 | 18 |
| 19 | 20 | 21 | 22 | 23 | 24 | 25 |
| 26 | 27 | 28 | 29 | 30 | | |

## 29
SUNDAY

## 30
MONDAY

KIKI CUYLER
BORN 1899

TED WILLIAMS
BORN 1918

## 31
TUESDAY

EDDIE PLANK
BORN 1875

FRANK ROBINSON
BORN 1935

RAY DANDRIDGE
BORN 1913

## 1
WEDNESDAY

## 2
THURSDAY

ALBERT SPALDING
BORN 1850

## 3
FRIDAY

## 4
SATURDAY

THE mental and physical sides of education are given equal weight in an exquisite stained-glass window from around 1910, hand-painted by Franz Mayer of Munich, Germany. The portion shown is 4′6″ by 5′4″; the entire window measures 7′9″ by 13′6″. The upper portion shows the head and wings of a guardian angel. It originally decorated a parochial school in upstate New York.

### SEPTEMBER

| S | M | T | W | T | F | S |
|---|---|---|---|---|---|---|
|   |   |   | 1 | 2 | 3 | 4 |
| 5 | 6 | 7 | 8 | 9 | 10 | 11 |
| 12 | 13 | 14 | 15 | 16 | 17 | 18 |
| 19 | 20 | 21 | 22 | 23 | 24 | 25 |
| 26 | 27 | 28 | 29 | 30 |   |   |

## 5
SUNDAY

NAP LAJOIE
BORN 1874

## 6
MONDAY     LABOR DAY

RED FABER
BORN 1888

## 7
TUESDAY

## 8
WEDNESDAY

BUCK LEONARD
BORN 1907

FRANK CHANCE
BORN 1877

## 9
THURSDAY

FRANK FRISCH
BORN 1898

WAITE HOYT
BORN 1899

JOE MORGAN
BORN 1943

## 10
FRIDAY

HIGH POCKETS KELLY
BORN 1895

## 11
SATURDAY

**L**OST
CHANCE? Joe Tinker
tosses to Johnny
Evers, who prepares
to fire on to Frank
Chance and complete
the double play. The
slick-fielding trio's
heroics often moved
opposing fans to
despair, never more
eloquently than in
Franklin P. Adams's
famous 1910 verse,
which forever linked
the three in the minds
of fans. Despite their
close cooperation on
the field, Tinker and
Evers stopped
speaking to each
other in about 1907,
following a private
dispute with murky
origins.

# SEPTEMBER 1993

| SEPTEMBER | | | | | | |
|---|---|---|---|---|---|---|
| S | M | T | W | T | F | S |
| | | | 1 | 2 | 3 | 4 |
| 5 | 6 | 7 | 8 | 9 | 10 | 11 |
| 12 | 13 | 14 | 15 | 16 | 17 | 18 |
| 19 | 20 | 21 | 22 | 23 | 24 | 25 |
| 26 | 27 | 28 | 29 | 30 | | |

## 12
SUNDAY     GRANDPARENTS DAY

## 13
MONDAY

## 14
TUESDAY

**KID NICHOLS
BORN 1869**

## 15
WEDNESDAY

**GAYLORD PERRY
BORN 1938**

## 16
THURSDAY     ROSH HASHANAH

## 17
FRIDAY

**RUBE FOSTER
BORN 1879**

## 18
SATURDAY

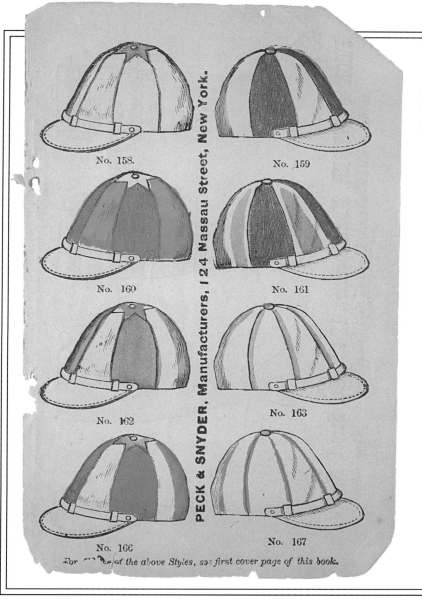

No. 158.

No. 159

No. 160

No. 161

No. 162

No. 163

No. 166

No. 167

PECK & SNYDER, Manufacturers, 124 Nassau Street, New York.

For some of the above Styles, see first cover page of this book.

**A** page from a nineteenth-century catalogue displays the baseball-cap fashions of the day.

# SEPTEMBER 1993

## SEPTEMBER

| S | M | T | W | T | F | S |
|---|---|---|---|---|---|---|
|   |   |   | 1 | 2 | 3 | 4 |
| 5 | 6 | 7 | 8 | 9 | 10 | 11 |
| 12 | 13 | 14 | 15 | 16 | 17 | 18 |
| 19 | 20 | 21 | 22 | 23 | 24 | 25 |
| 26 | 27 | 28 | 29 | 30 |   |   |

## 19
SUNDAY

**DUKE SNIDER
BORN 1926**

## 20
MONDAY

## 21
TUESDAY

## 22
WEDNESDAY

**BOB LEMON
BORN 1920**

## 23
THURSDAY

## 24
FRIDAY

## 25
SATURDAY

**YOM KIPPUR**

JOHN FALTER

**S**T. LOUIS fans appreciated Stan "the Man" Musial's 475 home runs and .331 lifetime average, but he was (and still is) equally beloved for his sunny and generous disposition. He batted and threw left-handed, but in this 1954 painting for a *Saturday Evening Post* cover by John Falter he performs another essential baseball activity—signing autographs— from the right side.

# SEPT / OCT 1993

OCTOBER

| S | M | T | W | T | F | S |
|---|---|---|---|---|---|---|
|   |   |   |   |   | 1 | 2 |
| 3 | 4 | 5 | 6 | 7 | 8 | 9 |
| 10 | 11 | 12 | 13 | 14 | 15 | 16 |
| 17 | 18 | 19 | 20 | 21 | 22 | 23 |
| 24/31 | 25 | 26 | 27 | 28 | 29 | 30 |

## 26
SUNDAY

## 27
MONDAY

## 28
TUESDAY

## 29
WEDNESDAY

**ROBIN ROBERTS**
**BORN 1926**

## 30
THURSDAY

## 1
FRIDAY

**RON CAREW**
**BORN 1945**

## 2
SATURDAY

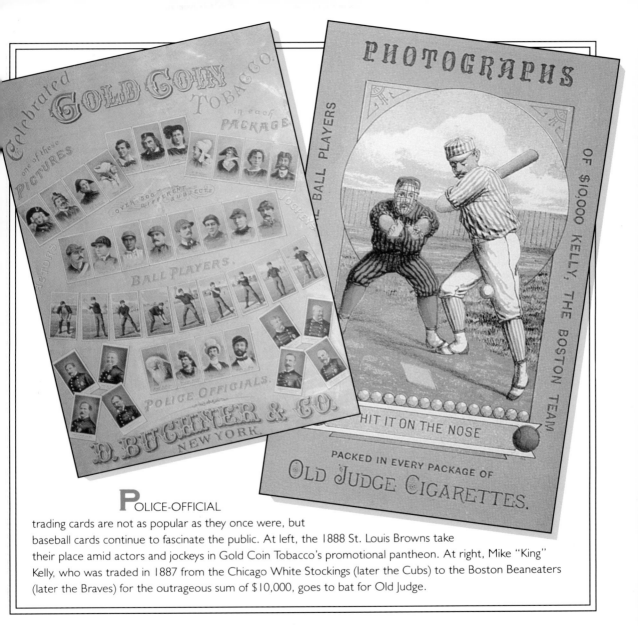

**P**OLICE-OFFICIAL trading cards are not as popular as they once were, but baseball cards continue to fascinate the public. At left, the 1888 St. Louis Browns take their place amid actors and jockeys in Gold Coin Tobacco's promotional pantheon. At right, Mike "King" Kelly, who was traded in 1887 from the Chicago White Stockings (later the Cubs) to the Boston Beaneaters (later the Braves) for the outrageous sum of $10,000, goes to bat for Old Judge.

# OCTOBER 1993

## OCTOBER
| S | M | T | W | T | F | S |
|---|---|---|---|---|---|---|
|   |   |   |   |   | 1 | 2 |
| 3 | 4 | 5 | 6 | 7 | 8 | 9 |
| 10 | 11 | 12 | 13 | 14 | 15 | 16 |
| 17 | 18 | 19 | 20 | 21 | 22 | 23 |
| 24/31 | 25 | 26 | 27 | 28 | 29 | 30 |

## 3
SUNDAY

## 4
MONDAY

## 5
TUESDAY

HENRY CHADWICK
BORN 1824

## 6
WEDNESDAY

## 7
THURSDAY

 CHUCK KLEIN
BORN 1904

## 8
FRIDAY

## 9
SATURDAY

RUBE MARQUARD
BORN 1889

JOE SEWELL
BORN 1898

**A** decorative pillow cover from around 1907 makes visual puns on such baseball terms as a star pitcher and a safe hit.

**OCTOBER**

| S | M | T | W | T | F | S |
|---|---|---|---|---|---|---|
|   |   |   |   |   | 1 | 2 |
| 3 | 4 | 5 | 6 | 7 | 8 | 9 |
| 10 | 11 | 12 | 13 | 14 | 15 | 16 |
| 17 | 18 | 19 | 20 | 21 | 22 | 23 |
| 24/31 | 25 | 26 | 27 | 28 | 29 | 30 |

## 10
SUNDAY

## 11
MONDAY

**COLUMBUS DAY OBSERVED**
**THANKSGIVING (CANADA)**

RICK FERRELL
BORN 1905

## 12
TUESDAY

**TRADITIONAL COLUMBUS DAY**

JOE CRONIN
BORN 1906

## 13
WEDNESDAY

RUBE WADDELL
BORN 1876
EDDIE MATHEWS
BORN 1931

## 14
THURSDAY

OSCAR CHARLESTON
BORN 1896

## 15
FRIDAY

JIM PALMER
BORN 1947

## 16
SATURDAY

WILL HARRIDGE
BORN 1883
HAPPY CHANDLER
BORN 1898
GOOSE GOSLIN
BORN 1900

**U**NION SOLDIERS in the Civil War take a break from killing Rebels to pose with the matériel of their other favorite sport.

# OCTOBER 1993

**OCTOBER**

| S | M | T | W | T | F | S |
|---|---|---|---|---|---|---|
|   |   |   |   |   | 1 | 2 |
| 3 | 4 | 5 | 6 | 7 | 8 | 9 |
| 10 | 11 | 12 | 13 | 14 | 15 | 16 |
| 17 | 18 | 19 | 20 | 21 | 22 | 23 |
| 24/31 | 25 | 26 | 27 | 28 | 29 | 30 |

## 17
SUNDAY

**BUCK EWING**
**BORN 1859**

## 18
MONDAY

**CANDY CUMMINGS**
**BORN 1848**

## 19
TUESDAY

**MORDECAI BROWN**
**BORN 1876**

## 20
WEDNESDAY

**MICKEY MANTLE**
**BORN 1931**

**JUAN MARICHAL**
**BORN 1937**

## 21
THURSDAY

**WHITEY FORD**
**BORN 1928**

## 22
FRIDAY

**JIMMIE FOXX**
**BORN 1907**

## 23
SATURDAY

**B**ASEBALL is usually a noncontact sport, but every now and then one sees a fierce collision on the diamond. Gregory A. Miller depicted the ever-popular play at home plate in *Big League*, from around 1940.

# OCTOBER 1993

| S | M | T | W | T | F | S |
|---|---|---|---|---|---|---|
| | | | | | 1 | 2 |
| 3 | 4 | 5 | 6 | 7 | 8 | 9 |
| 10 | 11 | 12 | 13 | 14 | 15 | 16 |
| 17 | 18 | 19 | 20 | 21 | 22 | 23 |
| 24/31 | 25 | 26 | 27 | 28 | 29 | 30 |

## 24
### SUNDAY

## 25
### MONDAY

**LARRY MacPHAIL**
**BORN 1917**

## 26
### TUESDAY

**WILLIAM (JUDY)**
**JOHNSON**
**BORN 1899**

## 27
### WEDNESDAY

**RALPH KINER**
**BORN 1922**

## 28
### THURSDAY

## 29
### FRIDAY

## 30
### SATURDAY

**ED DELAHANTY**
**BORN 1867**

**BILL TERRY**
**BORN 1898**

THE close play at home is baseball at its most violent, and a perennial favorite of artists. Here the medium is a tin plate from the 1920s or 1930s, painted with a scene in which the catcher has discarded his mask which better displays his youthful features.

**NOVEMBER**

| S | M | T | W | T | F | S |
|---|---|---|---|---|---|---|
|   | 1 | 2 | 3 | 4 | 5 | 6 |
| 7 | 8 | 9 | 10 | 11 | 12 | 13 |
| 14 | 15 | 16 | 17 | 18 | 19 | 20 |
| 21 | 22 | 23 | 24 | 25 | 26 | 27 |
| 28 | 29 | 30 |   |   |   |   |

## 31
SUNDAY          HALLOWEEN

FRED CLARKE
BORN 1872

CAL HUBBARD
BORN 1900

## 1
MONDAY

## 2
TUESDAY          ELECTION DAY

TRAVIS JACKSON
BORN 1903

## 3
WEDNESDAY

BOB FELLER
BORN 1918

## 4
THURSDAY

BOBBY WALLACE
BORN 1874

## 5
FRIDAY

## 6
SATURDAY

WALTER JOHNSON
BORN 1887

**R**OBERT RAUSCHENBERG adopts his usual eclectic approach in a 1979 silkscreen and collage entitled *Back Out*.

# NOVEMBER 1993

NOVEMBER
S M T W T F S
1 2 3 4 5 6
7 8 9 10 11 12 13
14 15 16 17 18 19 20
21 22 23 24 25 26 27
28 29 30

## 7
SUNDAY

## 8
MONDAY

**BUCKY HARRIS
BORN 1896**

## 9
TUESDAY

**BOB GIBSON
BORN 1935**

## 10
WEDNESDAY

## 11
THURSDAY

**VETERANS DAY
REMEMBRANCE DAY (CANADA)**

**RABBIT MARANVILLE
BORN 1891**

**PIE TRAYNOR
BORN 1899**

## 12
FRIDAY

## 13
SATURDAY

CASEY STENGEL presided over the greatest dynasty baseball has ever known. During his 12 years with the New York Yankees, from 1949 to 1960, the team won ten American League pennants and seven World Series. Here he directs his team against the Milwaukee Braves during the sixth game of the 1958 fall classic. The Yankees took that game in 10 innings and won again the next day to capture the series.

# NOVEMBER 1993

NOVEMBER

| S | M | T | W | T | F | S |
|---|---|---|---|---|---|---|
|   | 1 | 2 | 3 | 4 | 5 | 6 |
| 7 | 8 | 9 | 10 | 11 | 12 | 13 |
| 14 | 15 | 16 | 17 | 18 | 19 | 20 |
| 21 | 22 | 23 | 24 | 25 | 26 | 27 |
| 28 | 29 | 30 |   |   |   |   |

## 14
SUNDAY

## 15
MONDAY

## 16
TUESDAY

## 17
WEDNESDAY

**THOMAS EDWARD SEAVER
BORN 1944**

## 18
THURSDAY

## 19
FRIDAY

**ROY CAMPANELLA
BORN 1921**

## 20
SATURDAY

**KENESAW MOUNTAIN LANDIS
BORN 1866**

**CLARK GRIFFITH
BORN 1869**

**P**LAY-at-home baseball games are nearly as old as the sport itself. There have been variations using dice, cards, dart boards, and now computers. In this game, issued in the late 19th century by McLoughlin Brothers, a spinner and pegboard control the game's progress—less arbitrary, to be sure, than the baseball gods often are in real life.

NOVEMBER

| S | M | T | W | T | F | S |
|---|---|---|---|---|---|---|
|   | 1 | 2 | 3 | 4 | 5 | 6 |
| 7 | 8 | 9 | 10 | 11 | 12 | 13 |
| 14 | 15 | 16 | 17 | 18 | 19 | 20 |
| 21 | 22 | 23 | 24 | 25 | 26 | 27 |
| 28 | 29 | 30 |   |   |   |   |

## 21
SUNDAY

**FRED LINDSTROM**
**BORN 1905**

**STAN MUSIAL**
**BORN 1920**

## 22
MONDAY

## 23
TUESDAY

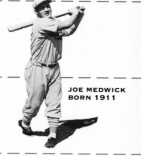

**JOE MEDWICK**
**BORN 1911**

## 24
WEDNESDAY

## 25
THURSDAY

**THANKSGIVING**

**JOE DiMAGGIO**
**BORN 1914**

## 26
FRIDAY

**HUGH DUFFY**
**BORN 1866**

**LEFTY GOMEZ**
**BORN 1908**

## 27
SATURDAY

**U**NIFORMS no longer look like the late-19th-century one this young man is wearing, and nowadays home plate has five sides. But some things never change; showing fine form on the diamond is still an excellent way to impress the ladies, though today they may not be as demure as the ones pictured.

# NOV/DEC 1993

| DECEMBER | | | | | | |
|---|---|---|---|---|---|---|
| S | M | T | W | T | F | S |
| | | | 1 | 2 | 3 | 4 |
| 5 | 6 | 7 | 8 | 9 | 10 | 11 |
| 12 | 13 | 14 | 15 | 16 | 17 | 18 |
| 19 | 20 | 21 | 22 | 23 | 24 | 25 |
| 26 | 27 | 28 | 29 | 30 | 31 | |

## 28
SUNDAY

## 29
MONDAY

## 30
TUESDAY

## 1
WEDNESDAY

WALTER ALSTON
BORN 1911

## 2
THURSDAY

## 3
FRIDAY

## 4
SATURDAY

JESSE BURKETT
BORN 1868

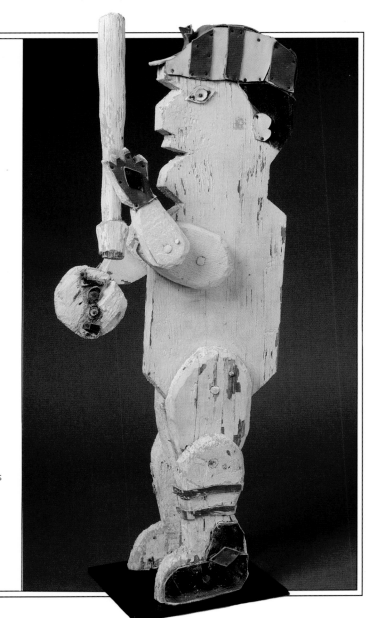

**B**ASEBALL has always been a fertile subject for folk art. It's not clear what the undated *Articulated Baseball Figure* by an anonymous whittler was used for, but this two-foot-tall polychrome piece was operated with strings.

**DECEMBER**

| S | M | T | W | T | F | S |
|---|---|---|---|---|---|---|
|   |   |   | 1 | 2 | 3 | 4 |
| 5 | 6 | 7 | 8 | 9 | 10 | 11 |
| 12 | 13 | 14 | 15 | 16 | 17 | 18 |
| 19 | 20 | 21 | 22 | 23 | 24 | 25 |
| 26 | 27 | 28 | 29 | 30 | 31 |   |

**5**
SUNDAY

**6**
MONDAY

JOCKO CONLAN
BORN 1899

TONY LAZZERI
BORN 1903

**7**
TUESDAY

JOHNNY BENCH
BORN 1947

**8**
WEDNESDAY

**9**
THURSDAY          HANUKKAH

JOE KELLEY
BORN 1871

**10**
FRIDAY

**11**
SATURDAY

CHARLES RADBOURN
BORN 1854

**R**OGERS HORNSBY was the best-hitting second baseman of all time. He led the National League seven times in batting average, twice in home runs, and four times in RBIs. He was an enormous asset to any club, but his fiery temperament, disregard for authority, and salary demands that were ahead of his time caused him to be traded frequently. Here he is seen in his first game for the Chicago Cubs, a spring-training contest against the Los Angeles Angels of the Pacific Coast League in 1929.

# DECEMBER 1993

| DECEMBER | | | | | | |
|---|---|---|---|---|---|---|
| S | M | T | W | T | F | S |
|  |  |  | 1 | 2 | 3 | 4 |
| 5 | 6 | 7 | 8 | 9 | 10 | 11 |
| 12 | 13 | 14 | 15 | 16 | 17 | 18 |
| 19 | 20 | 21 | 22 | 23 | 24 | 25 |
| 26 | 27 | 28 | 29 | 30 | 31 |  |

## 12
SUNDAY

## 13
MONDAY

**FERGUSON JENKINS**
**BORN 1943**

## 14
TUESDAY

## 15
WEDNESDAY

## 16
THURSDAY

## 17
FRIDAY

## 18
SATURDAY

**TY COBB**
**BORN 1886**

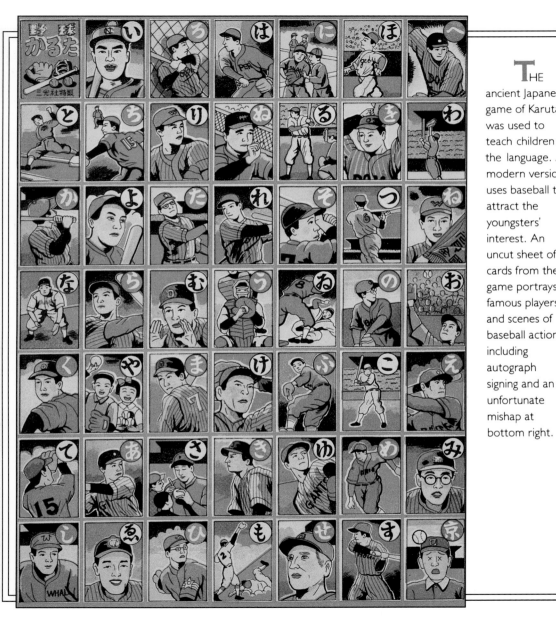

THE ancient Japanese game of Karuta was used to teach children the language. A modern version uses baseball to attract the youngsters' interest. An uncut sheet of cards from the game portrays famous players and scenes of baseball action, including autograph signing and an unfortunate mishap at bottom right.

# D E C E M B E R   1 9 9 3

DECEMBER

| S | M | T | W | T | F | S |
|---|---|---|---|---|---|---|
|   |   |   | 1 | 2 | 3 | 4 |
| 5 | 6 | 7 | 8 | 9 | 10 | 11 |
| 12 | 13 | 14 | 15 | 16 | 17 | 18 |
| 19 | 20 | 21 | 22 | 23 | 24 | 25 |
| 26 | 27 | 28 | 29 | 30 | 31 |   |

## 19
SUNDAY

**FORD FRICK BORN 1894**
**AL KALINE BORN 1934**

## 20
MONDAY

**BRANCH RICKEY BORN 1881**

**GABBY HARTNETT BORN 1900**

## 21
TUESDAY

**JOSH GIBSON BORN 1911**

## 22
WEDNESDAY

**CONNIE MACK BORN 1862**

## 23
THURSDAY

## 24
FRIDAY

## 25
SATURDAY   **CHRISTMAS**

**PUD GALVIN BORN 1856**

**C**LAES OLDENBURG, a larger-than-life figure in the Pop Art movement, created *Bat Spinning at the Speed of Light,* a lithograph, in 1975. If an announcer says that a slugger has pop in his bat, he is probably an Oldenburg fan.

# D E C E M B E R   1 9 9 3

**DECEMBER**

| S | M | T | W | T | F | S |
|---|---|---|---|---|---|---|
|   |   |   | 1 | 2 | 3 | 4 |
| 5 | 6 | 7 | 8 | 9 | 10 | 11 |
| 12 | 13 | 14 | 15 | 16 | 17 | 18 |
| 19 | 20 | 21 | 22 | 23 | 24 | 25 |
| 26 | 27 | 28 | 29 | 30 | 31 |   |

**26**
SUNDAY    BOXING DAY (CANADA)

MORGAN BULKELEY
BORN 1837

**27**
MONDAY

**28**
TUESDAY

TED LYONS
BORN 1900

**29**
WEDNESDAY

**30**
THURSDAY

SANDY KOUFAX
BORN 1935

**31**
FRIDAY

MIKE KELLY
BORN 1857

TOMMY CONNOLLY
BORN 1870

CONTROVERSY rages to this day over whether Babe Ruth "called his shot" before homering off Charlie Root of the Chicago Cubs in the 1932 World Series. Eyewitnesses agree that he made some sort of gesture before his mighty blow, but it was certainly not as dramatic as illustrated here, in an advertisement for toiletries. Whatever the facts of the matter, the episode has become one of baseball's most enduring myths.

# C R E D I T S

**8/29-9/4** Gladstone Collection of Baseball Art, photographed by Eric Landsberg.

**9/5-9/11** National Baseball Library.
**9/12-9/18** Thomas Carwile Collection.
**9/19-9/25** National Baseball Library, © Curtis Publishing Company.
**9/26-10/2** Kenneth R. Felden Collection.

**10/3-10/9, 10/10-10/16, & 10/17-10/23** Gladstone Collection of Baseball Art.
**10/24-10/30** Gladstone Collection of Baseball Art, photographed by Eric Landsberg.
**10/31-11/6** Gladstone Collection of Baseball Art, photographed by Eric Landsberg, © Robert Rauschenberg/VAGA, N.Y

**11/7-11/13** Wide World Photos, Inc.
**11/14-11/20** Kenneth R. Felden Collection.
**11/21-11/27** Gladstone Collection of Baseball Art, photographed by Eric Landsberg.
**11/28-12/4** Gladstone Collection of Baseball Art, photographed by Sheldan Collins.

**12/5-12/11** Wide World Photos, Inc.
**12/12-12/18** Gladstone Collection of Baseball Art, photographed by Eric Landsberg.
**12/19-12/25** Gladstone Collection of Baseball Art, © Landfall Press, New York City.
**12/26-1/1** Thomas Carwile Collection.

**NOTES PAGE**
Gladstone Collection of Baseball Art, photographed by Sheldan Collins.

**ACKNOWLEDGMENTS**
Pictures of the following players are used with the permission of the Curtis Management Group, Indianapolis, Ind.: Grover Cleveland Alexander, Ty Cobb, Mickey Cochrane, Dizzy Dean, Bob Feller, Lou Gehrig, Lefty Grove, Gil Hodges, Rogers Hornsby, Monte Irvin, Harmon Killebrew, Ralph Kiner, Billy Martin, Christy Mathewson, Johnny Mize, Edd Roush, Babe Ruth, Tris Speaker, Casey Stengel, Honus Wagner, and Cy Young.

Very special thanks to Mr. and Mrs. William Gladstone. Thanks also to Ken Felden, Thomas Carwile, Patricia Kelly at the National Baseball Library, and Eric Landsberg and Craig Phillips.

# HALL OF FAMERS 1939-1992

## PIONEERS & EXECUTIVES

Ed Barrow
Morgan Bulkeley
Alexander Cartwright
Henry Chadwick
Albert B. (Happy) Chandler
Charles Comiskey
William Arthur (Candy) Cummings
Ford Frick
Warren Giles
Clark Griffith
Will Harridge
Byron Bancroft (Ban) Johnson
Kenesaw Mountain Landis
Leland (Larry) Macphail
Wesley (Branch) Rickey
Albert Spalding
Bill Veeck
George Weiss
George Wright
Harry Wright
Thomas Austin (Tom) Yawkey

## MANAGERS

Walter Alston
Stanley Raymond (Bucky) Harris
Miller Huggins
Al Lopez
Connie Mack
Joe McCarthy
John McGraw
Bill McKechnie
Wilbert Robinson
Charles Dillon (Casey) Stengel

## PITCHERS

Grover Cleveland Alexander
Charles Albert (Chief) Bender
Mordecai (Three-Finger) Brown
Jack Chesbro
John Clarkson
Stan Coveleski
Jay Hanna (Dizzy) Dean
Don Drysdale
Urban Clarence (Red) Faber
Bob Feller
Roland Glen Fingers
Edward Charles (Whitey) Ford
James Francis (Pud) Galvin
Bob Gibson
Vernon Louis (Lefty) Gomez
Burleigh Grimes
Robert Moses (Lefty) Grove
Jesse Haines
Waite Hoyt
Carl Hubbell
James Augustus (Catfish) Hunter
Ferguson Jenkins
Walter Johnson
Adrian (Addie) Joss
Tim Keefe
Sandy Koufax
Bob Lemon
Ted Lyons
Juan Marichal
Richard Williams (Rube) Marquard
Christy Mathewson
Joe McGinnity
Harold Newhouser
Charles August (Kid) Nichols
Jim Palmer
Herb Pennock
Gaylord Perry
Eddie Plank
Charles Radbourn
Eppa Rixey
Robin Roberts
Charles Herbert (Red) Ruffing
Amos Rusie
Thomas Edward Seaver
Warren Spahn
Clarence Arthur (Dazzy) Vance
George Edward (Rube) Waddell

# HALL OF FAMERS 1939 - 1992

Edward Augustine (Ed) Walsh
Mickey Welch
Hoyt Wilhelm
Early Wynn
Denton True (Cy) Young

## FIRST BASEMEN

Adian Constantine (Cap) Anson
Jake Beckley
Jim Bottomley
Dan Brouthers
Frank Chance
Roger Connor
Jimmie Fox
Ludwig Heinrich (Lou) Gehrig
Hank Greenberg
George Kell
Harmon Killebrew
Willie McCovey
Johnny Mize
George Sisler
Wilver Dornell (Willie) Stargell
Bill Terry

## SECOND BASEMEN

Rod Carew
Edward Trowbridge (Eddie) Collins

Bobby Doerr
Johnny Evers
Frank Frisch
Charley Gehringer
Billy Herman
Rogers Hornsby
Larry (Nap) Lajoie
Tony Lazzeri
Joe Morgan
Jackie Robinson
Albert Fred (Red) Schoendienst

## SHORTSTOPS

Luis Aparicio
Luke Appling
Dave Bancroft
Ernie Banks
Lou Boudreau
Joe Cronin
Travis Jackson
Hughey Jennings
Walter James Vincent
   (Rabbit) Maranville
Harold Henry (Pee-Wee)
   Reese
Joe Sewell
Joe Tinker
Joseph Floyd (Arky) Vaughan

Johannes Peter (Honus)
   Wagner
Roderick John (Bobby)
   Wallace
John Montgomery Ward

## THIRD BASEMEN

Frank (Home Run) Baker
Jimmy Collins
George (High Pockets) Kelly
Fred Lindstrom
Eddie Mathews
Brooks Robinson
Harold Joseph (Pie) Traynor

## CATCHERS

Johnny Bench
Lawrence Peter (Yogi) Berra
Roger Bresnahan
Roy Campanella
Gordon Stanley (Mickey)
   Cochrane
Bill Dickey
William (Buck) Ewing
Rick Ferrell
Gabby Hartnett
Ernie Lombardi
Ray Schalk

# HALL OF FAMERS 1939-1992

## LEFT FIELDERS

Lou Brock
Jesse Burkett
Fred Clarke
Ed Delahanty
Leon Allen (Goose) Goslin
Charles James (Chick) Hafey
Joe Kelley
Ralph Kiner
Henry Emmett (Heinie)
   Manush
Joe Medwick
Stan Musial
Jim O'Rourke
Al Simmons
Zack Wheat
Billy Williams
Ted Williams
Carl Yastrzemski

## CENTER FIELDERS

Howard (Earl) Averill
Maximilian Carnarius (Max)
   Carey
Tyrus Raymond (Ty) Cobb
Earle Combs
Joe DiMaggio
Hugh Duffy

Billy Hamilton
Mickey Mantle
Willie Mays
Edd Roush
Edwin Donald (Duke) Snider
Tris Speaker
Lloyd Waner
Louis Robert (Hack) Wilson

## RIGHT FIELDERS

Henry Louis (Hank) Aaron
Roberto Clemente
Sam Crawford
Hazen Shirley (Kiki) Cuyler
Elmer Flick
Harry Heilmann
Harry Hooper
Al Kaline
Willie Keeler
Mike Kelly
Chuck Klein
Tommy McCarthy
Mel Ott
Edgar (Sam) Rice
Frank Robinson
George Herman (Babe) Ruth
Enos Slaughter
Sam Thompson

Paul Waner
Royce Middlebrook (Ross)
   Youngs

## FROM NEGRO LEAGUES

James (Cool Papa) Bell
Oscar Charleston
Ray Dandridge
Martin Dihigo
George (Rube) Foster
Josh Gibson
Monte Irvin
William Julius (Judy)
   Johnson
Walter Fenner (Buck)
   Leonard
John Henry Lloyd
Leroy Robert (Satchel) Paige

## UMPIRES

Al Barlick
John (Jocko) Conlan
Tommy Connolly
Billy Evans
Robert (Cal) Hubbard
Bill Klem
Bill McGowan

_____
_____
_____
_____
_____
_____
_____
_____
_____
_____
_____
_____
_____

# NOTES

# NOTES

# NOTES